To
Become
a
Human
Being

Also by Steve Wall

Travels in a Stone Canoe
(with Harvey Arden)

Dancing with God: Americans Who Have Been Touched by the Divine

Shadowcatchers: Journey in Search of Native American Healers

Wisdom's Daughters: Conversations with Native American Women Elders

Wisdomkeepers: Meetings with Native American Spiritual Elders
(with Harvey Arden)

Appalachian Life

Love on the Line
(with Walker L. Knight)

To
Become
a
Human
Being

| The Message of | Tadodaho Chief | Leon Shenandoah | |

Steve Wall

HAMPTON ROADS
PUBLISHING COMPANY, INC.
for the evolving human spirit

Cover design by Jane Hagaman
Cover and interior photos by Steve Wall

Hampton Roads Publishing Company, Inc.
1125 Stoney Ridge Road
Charlottesville, VA 22902

434-296-2772
fax: 434-296-5096
e-mail: hrpc@hrpub.com
www.hrpub.com

If you are unable to order this book from your local
bookseller, you may order directly from the publisher.
Call 1-800-766-8009, toll-free.

Library of Congress Catalog Card Number: 2001092126

ISBN 978-1-57174-341-1

10 9 8 7 6 5 4 3 2

Printed on acid-free paper in the United States

Contents

Foreword

"When somebody dies, the spirit of that person lives on. Spirits can go and come from that place where the Creator lives. It's easier for them to go back and forth as long as somebody remembers them or there's important business they didn't get completed before they died. My Indian name means 'Unfinished Business.' I guess I'll have to do a lot of traveling after I leave this place and go to where the Creator is. There's always more to do.

"Some spirits stay here and don't go to be with the Creator. That's different than going and coming. Those who stay here are probably the ones who never tried to find the Creator while they were alive. They're the spirits that are trying to get back at somebody or they're up to no good by stirring up things. Some are just tied here and maybe don't know they're dead. But the spirits that travel are working for the good. They're not out to do harm.

"When I go, I'll not be wanting to leave. So I'll have some visiting to do. Look out! I may come to see you.

"You know what I told you, 'Pay attention. And listen. There really is no death.'"

Leon was back for a visit. He said he would be returning. He always kept his word. The Chief had been to my home numerous times over the years since our first meeting in 1984. At the time, I was on a *National Geographic* assignment covering the Iroquois Confederacy. When I arrived at Onondaga, the confederacy's capital just south of Syracuse, New York, there was a lot going on. Dennis Banks, the fugitive American Indian movement leader who had been given sanctuary there, was preparing to return to South Dakota in order to turn himself in. Because I was a photographer, I was asked by one of the chiefs to take pictures of him to prove he was in good physical condition before his surrender. Gladly, I obliged.

When I finished, an older gentleman, who had been asked to pose alongside of Dennis, came forward with his hand outstretched. Up until that time he had been very quiet, content to sit pretty much in the background and puff on his old pipe. Now he was in front of me, not saying a word, hand palm up as if asking for something. The chief who had orchestrated the affair introduced me to the Tadodaho, Chief Leon Shenandoah. And I was to give him my film for safekeeping until the whole affair was over. This was to ensure that I wouldn't release it to the news media, since Dennis would be secretly traveling to South Dakota.

I didn't know who Chief Leon Shenandoah was, and I certainly didn't know what the word "Tadodaho" meant. One thing I did know. Giving up my film was out of the question. I had never, ever, handed over my film to anyone before. Not in war, not when confronted by security forces in other countries, never. Now, this kindly elder was not asking, he was simply making it clear. I had to give him the film. And I did. Freely.

Chief Leon Shenandoah never said a word. He didn't have to. As strange as it was to me at the time, I trusted him completely. Our friendship had begun.

Over the next twelve years Leon and I became very close. Even after my assignment ended, we traveled to various places together and visited each other often. When we weren't doing something together, we would, at the very least, stay in touch by phone and catch up on all the happenings in each of our lives. We would laugh and laugh throughout each conversation. We were friends. And as it is with friends, we knew each other well.

Everyone who knows me, and Leon was no exception, is aware that I work late, sometimes into the wee hours of the morning. It's just about an every-night affair. Then, I go to bed and sleep my eight hours, meaning I'm a slow riser. My routine was no different on the eve before Leon's arrival. But for some reason I was up early the next morning with only about four hours sleep. Trying to shake the drowsiness from my sleepy head, I made my way downstairs. Just as I entered my office, and before I was completely through the door, a cool breeze rushed past me. It gave me a mild chill. I was awake! And the thought of Leon replaced my wonder of being up so early. Crossing the threshold I immediately went to my bookcase and began searching for a poster Leon had signed years earlier. Being a little impulsive and slightly obsessive, I never questioned why, I was just doing it.

Finding the rolled up poster behind a row of books relating to Native Americans, I grabbed for it. In so doing, I dislodged a stack of papers crammed between two titles. The phone rang. I jumped and out spilled page after page of scribbled notes. As I picked up the phone, I glanced down to see my notes of interviews I had done over the years with Leon. With a "hello," I bent to pick up a sheet here and there. Then I heard the fateful message. "Leon just died a few minutes ago."

For a few seconds I couldn't say a word. I just held the phone as my eyes moved first to the poster now in front of me on my desk and the pile of paper strewn all over the floor at my feet. Leon! My mind raced between a rapidly rising sadness and an overpowering awe.

Could it be? Leon here! Could he already be traveling just as he said he would? And in my home, in my study? Here with me? I was definitely now fully awake.

After hanging up the phone, I began to gather up the pages containing Leon's words. In 1992, Leon and I had a conversation about my doing a book about his way of life and philosophy for living. About becoming "a human being," as he put it. At the time, he signed a release giving me permission to do it. Because of his position as Tadodaho, he knew he wouldn't be able to do it himself. Because of political issues surrounding Leon at that time, we were not able to do the book. Time after time we talked and I made notes. We traveled a lot together, to New York City, London, upstate New York, Six Nations Reserve near Hamilton, Ontario, and Wounded Knee. Numerous times he visited my wife and me in North Carolina. Once he was in our home for Thanksgiving, and it truly was a Thanksgiving dinner my family will never forget. Leon was always eager to come for a visit, and more than eager to travel. It was obvious that Leon enjoyed going anywhere. It didn't matter where. Just go. But he always made it a point to talk to me about the things that were important to him. Often he would scold me to "pay attention."

"Remember," he would say. Then, from time to time, he would remind me of "the book."

When I would get distracted taking pictures during our travels or tied up doing something around the house, he would engage my wife, B.J. Although he and I were very close, he did not discriminate between men and women. Each was equal to him. So it was with B.J. that he shared issues that were important to him. Once he learned of my wife's abilities in dealing with spiritual matters and her familiarity with higher spirits, he turned to her with questions he needed answering relating to that realm, just as he had gone to "Daisy," his longtime spiritual adviser, for answers. Leon and B.J. developed a tight bond. We were members of the same family without having come from the same bloodline.

Leon became my teacher from the first day we met. We both knew it. Neither of us had to voice it. The connection had been made. And he still is my mentor. I hear his words today just as plainly as I did so many years ago. It's as if he is sitting beside me now and saying them for the first time. I see him in my mind's eye as clearly as I did when we were together.

Leon was a small man, but no one knew it. He had stature. And he had an aura around him that drew people to him. When he entered a room filled with people, everyone would turn instinctively toward him without knowing why. What they saw was a man with silky white hair pulled back into a ponytail. His usual attire was a plaid shirt, jeans, and tennis shoes, unless he was wearing the Iroquois ribbon shirt reserved for official occasions. He wore it when he addressed the United Nations, met presidents, or spoke to diplomats about human rights and environmental issues.

By most standards Leon was a poor man. He had little or no money. But he never took any thought of where he would sleep, how he would eat, or how he would get to where he was intending to go. Yet, he never missed a night's sleep for lack of a place to stay. He never had to skip a meal. And he always reached his destination. His simple knowing that the Creator would take care of him if he was on his mission made him the richest man I ever knew. He walked his path; his needs were always met.

So many people were touched by his presence. He touched even those who did not know him personally. He was a peacemaker. In this society the warrior is portrayed as the hero, yet this one small man could take the warrior out of the most belligerent with his gentleness. He gave us the words, "The greatest strength is in gentleness." Make no mistake about it, gentleness to him did not mean weakness. It was the ultimate strength. There was no weapon against it, because gentleness came from spirituality.

Warriors are held up as heroes. They are praised for their gallantry, exalted for their conquests, and used as symbols to inspire patriotism. Monuments are built for them as reminders of past victories and to prepare citizens for the next campaign. Leon Shenandoah was no warrior, yet no warrior could stand up against his power. He carried no weapons, used no harsh rhetoric, and made no demands. His strength was in gentleness. When he spoke, those around him listened. His words were always soft, his kindness evident. He was a spiritual man.

Leon never said an unkind word about anyone. He would talk about issues, but he would never name the names of those who were trying to sway people's opinions. When anyone would ask him a leading question about political events, he would handle the situation calmly. He would take out his old pipe, pack it with tobacco, fire it up and puff a time or two. Then he would simply sit there. Silence would fill the room. While the questioner waited for an answer, Leon would fire the pipe again and draw the smoke. And he would sit there, staring out the window or into a blank wall. That was his answer; it was no answer but it was as powerful as any. He wasn't going to speak if it meant talking about someone. It was that simple. Next question.

In 1969, Leon was given the daunting office of Tadodaho, spiritual leader of the Six Nations. So began his tenure of working for the benefit of all the people. To him, this literally meant "all the people": all of the Creator's people wherever on earth they may be. This was not only his path—it was his mission. The medicine woman who attended him as a toddler had foreseen this position of "high office" for which the Creator was saving him. He took the position seriously; however, it was merely an extension of who he was and what he came into this world to do. He came for the benefit of all the people. As long as he lived, he never lost sight of his purpose. He served the people, all of us, well.

He taught us that becoming a "human being" was to reach the highest level in this life. Leon felt that to be a "human being" was more than just being human. It was to rise above instincts or emotions and reach a place of recognizing that we all are spiritual beings. And being spiritual was to acknowledge the Creator in every aspect of daily living. It was to commune with the Creator and listen as the Creator whispered back. Leon did this with every breath he took. And with each breath, he gave thanks. He never asked the Creator for anything because everything had been provided. Further, he said on many occasions that the Creator gave every human a mind and that by using the "good mind" each person would have the wisdom to make correct decisions, no matter the situation. For Leon, there were no problems, only opportunities.

He taught us that being a "human being" is our highest attainment. Even the animals don't do to each other what humans do. Animals are just doing their duty. They aren't wild; they were free. And so are we. We can do whatever we want, but being a "human being" means we show respect for each other and for all the other kingdoms. Some people try to separate us from what many of us call nature. There is no word for nature in Leon's language. We are all part of what is called nature. We're just one part of the whole. And "human beings" must give thanks.

When asked how one would know if another was a "human being" or not, Leon would say, "You just know. They know the Creator. They work for the benefit of the people, and they walk so softly on Mother Earth they don't even leave any footprints."

Today there are no visible signs of Leon Shenandoah's having been on this earth, but he left more than footprints. He left a place in my heart, just as he did in the hearts of everyone who ever met him or knew him. And for me, just as there must be for the multitudes who knew him, there is not one day that goes by without my thinking of him.

Leon lived his spirituality. He had no need to profess it. He was draped in it. It surrounded him. It flowed from within and touched everyone who ever met him. Of all the individuals I ever met, he was the only one who truly walked the spiritual path.

When I find myself feeling a little sad, he comes to mind. I think of how much he loved living, how thankful he was to be on this earth, and how much he enjoyed everything around him. Then I breathe deeply and thank him. My sadness lifts and I can almost hear him laugh his quiet laugh. That's when I whisper "Thank you" to him and the Creator for the honor of knowing him as a true friend and as Tadodaho. The world is a better place because of him.

Introduction

It is my privilege to introduce Steve Wall—writer, photographer, and author of this outstanding work. I first met Steve when he was on assignment for a *National Geographic* article about the American Indians, including Cherokee, of the southern Appalachian area of the Smokey and Blue Ridge Mountains, North Carolina, which is still alive in past cultural influence. We have shared a rich friendship for almost twenty years.

It was during this assignment, and perhaps because of the cultural influences he encountered, that Steve Wall set out on a different path. It was one that would change his life and work forever. His early perception of the philosophical depth of the traditional Indian wisdom-keepers created a passionate determination to preserve this timeless information for future generations. It was evident to him that the old traditions were dying out, and that the past and present influence of white culture, and in particular that of the United States government, had by design led the present generations of original Americans away from their traditional cultural heritage.

Steve, himself a native of North Carolina and part Cherokee, enthusiastically set out on the Blue Ridge assignment to achieve his goal of helping to preserve traditional wisdom. He did so without foreknowledge of the unbelievable, and at times seemingly impossible difficulties he would face in achieving his goal. I personally know of times when a less-determined writer would have given up, but he persevered. Today he is, in my opinion, one of the most qualified and prolific writers and photographers on the subject.

Wisdomkeepers, of which Wall is coauthor and photographer, was a literary and photographic success. It became an international bestseller, with hundreds of thousands of copies sold in this country and around the world. It has now been published in numerous foreign languages, including Japanese. Next he wrote and photographed *Wisdom's Daughters*, which explored the feminine influence and wisdom of the traditional Native American culture. These two books are perhaps the only record of the most traditional Native American elders living at that time.

Leon Shenandoah, the subject of this text, was featured in *Wisdomkeepers* and appeared on that book's cover. Chief Shenandoah was a true and authentic Native American elder and keeper of the wisdom. Thanks to Steve, I had the opportunity and privilege of knowing him personally and sharing with him for a number of years before his death in 1996. The Chief was a member of the Onondaga Nation, a sovereign nation just south of Syracuse in upper New York State, and one of the six nations that make up the Iroquois Confederacy. He was Tadodaho, an Iroquois office that is comparable to the Speaker of the House of Representatives. There is no position of president within their government, so this was a most high and venerated position.

He was one of the most humble, caring, and knowledgeable people concerning Indian tradition that I have ever met. He was also a spiritual giant. Physically he was not a big man, but in his presence, you had the impression that he was seven feet tall. He was not only a spiritual leader among his people but was a guiding spiritual force for multitudes around the world. He lived what he believed and was at home wherever he touched his Mother Earth.

When the Six Nations' lacrosse team was invited to a world championship game in Europe, there was a delay because of a downpour that lasted several hours. As the rain diminished to a drizzle, a small lone figure walked out onto a field covered with several inches of water. This followed the announcement that Chief Leon Shenandoah of the Six Nations would perform the ceremony of lighting the sacred fire. This ritual traditionally preceded the Indian game before the players entered the field of play and was for the purpose of giving thanks to the Creator, the provider of all things. As the smoke from the fire rose, the prayers of thanksgiving would rise into the heavens above. The crowd went silent, in part, perhaps, out of reverence, but mostly in awe of the impossible task that confronted the Chief. But Leon never wavered or hesitated. In the center of the field he knelt down upon his sacred Mother Earth and to the surprise and cheers of all, a small blaze soon sent smoke spiraling upward. Afterward, the battle between the Iroquois Nationals and Team England was fierce.

On another occasion, the State of New York planned to build an extra lane onto Interstate 81, which would have taken more Onondaga land against the wishes of the people. There was a confrontation between the Onondaga and the state police, who were sent by the governor to force the people back so that the bulldozers could continue the road-building project. Along with other chiefs, Leon held his ground. After several days of standoff, the police were sent to the prison at Attica to quell an uprising. The additional lanes were never completed, not even to this day.

Today, the physical presence of his honor, courage, and wisdom is gone, but his spirit lives on and is given rebirth and life in the pages of this book. Leon Shenandoah chose Steve Wall to write his story and Steve Wall chose to use the words recorded during the many hours spent with Leon to tell it. Any person remotely interested in spiritual matters and the wisdom of Native American elders, regardless of cultural background, will have a copy of this book in his or her library. It belongs in every public library in this nation, for it is truly a historic book that is destined to become a classic. Yes, Leon, Steve is putting your story in print. The world will come to know that there is "Strength in Gentleness."

Dr. J. Max Chastain
Philosopher and Mystic Healer
Southern Appalachia

The Creator must have worked on my mother's mind
when my name was given. It means "Unfinished Business."
Maybe He told them to give me that name
because someday I would be a leader. Lot of things that are not finished,
and when I leave they'll still be unfinished.
Everyone comes into this world with a mission.

"You pick the path that's yours
and the Creator
will show you your mission."

The Mission

I had mine, but I didn't know it when I was young.
When I was just so high, I was burned with boiling water.
My mother, everybody, thought I was going to die.
Somebody called a medicine woman and she doctored me.

She said that I was not going to die
because I was going to hold a very high position in the Confederacy.
I was going to have a lot of responsibility and help my people.
So they named me, in Indian,
a name that means something like Unfinished Business.
That's my name.

At the time I didn't understand, I was so young.
Nobody knew what the medicine woman meant by her prediction,
but she must have seen into the future.
Later, when I became an adult I went my own way.
I never paid much attention to what had
happened and what was said when I was a kid.
Then in my fifties I was made Tadodaho of the Six Nations.
Yes, the medicine woman saw ahead.
My mother told me later she figured I would become a faithkeeper
or maybe a chief of our clan.
The position of Tadodaho was not even considered.
I still have unfinished business because
there is so much to do for the people.

It is hard to know what your mission is when you're young.
Sometimes you can just barely see,
like an idea that you are here for something.
You get a feeling that you have more to do than just work and sleep.
It's a feeling. You don't dwell on it too much.
There are so many things that take your attention.
You act up and mess around. There are so many things to experience,
and life can seem to be hard at times. But then there's that feeling

like somebody's pulling at your shirt.
You've got to turn around and see what it is.
Maybe it's nothing, but it just won't go out of your mind.
You keep looking over your shoulder, to one side and the other.
But it's not behind you; it's out in front.
It's easier to look back than it is ahead.
But that's where your mission is waiting for you,
and that's where you've got to look.
When you finally get the courage to look that way
you can start to see. That's when it'll come to you.

Always look ahead.
You can see your path there and when you do,
then you can accept your mission.
You pick the path that's yours
and the Creator will show you your mission.
Your mission is always for the good of people.
If it doesn't benefit human beings and the Creation,
then it's not from the Creator. It's not your mission,
and you'd better double-check your path.
Your path is for your good,
and your mission is for the welfare of others.

When I was young I knew I was an Indian,
and I was treated differently because of it.
See, I went to city schools for two years, maybe.
My father wanted to move downtown
because he had to walk from Nedrow home
every night, every morning.
It was a long way and there were no taxis.
He had to walk to get down to the bus to go to work
and then walk back every evening. He had a hard time
because he couldn't read or write
and yet he knew more streets than I did.
He'd come back, scribble on a sign and give it to my mother,

telling the name of the street. He had to memorize it.
He knew more that way than I did.
He knew more streets from remembering.

He delivered coal to homes.
He worked for Kelly's coal yard right in Brighton for eighteen years.
He carried coal from the wagon to the houses.
That's what he did. He would dump the coal
down a chute that went to the cellar
and go back to the wagon for some more.
They had another guy that was shoveling.
When my father got back to the
wagon the other guy would have filled the next bag up.
From the wagon there was a little platform
that he would put the bag on and fill it up.
My father would grab the next bag
and put it on his shoulder and carry it to the chute and dump it.
He did that until he unloaded a ton of coal.

A long time ago, when people learned I was an Indian
they would say, "I'm sorry, but you're an Indian."
They said it to make me feel inferior.
I learned afterwards that I was a racist for a while.
But I learned from my elders
you must love all people that walk on this earth.
So I changed after I listened to the chiefs in the council talk
about being a racist.
Racism didn't come from the Indians. It came from the colonists.
Indians didn't know what a racist was.

There are some who are born with a special gift.
They were meant to help out the people in some way.
According to my mother, I had some special duty I guess.
I've been made a leader.

I was a faithkeeper before I was Tadodaho.
I was maybe in my late thirties then.
After that I was made Tadodaho.
The chiefs at Onondaga name the Tadodaho,
but the chiefs of the Six Nations have to approve it.
All the people have a voice in it.
There was a big gathering at the naming.
Nobody knew until that day except the chiefs of Onondaga.

I wasn't surprised
because I didn't have time to think about it
the way it happened.
It was presented to me after they met among themselves.
At the condolence
they had the roll call of the chiefs of the Six Nations,
and I was given the wampum string and the name that goes with it.
That name was Tadodaho.

Let me tell you about the original Tadodaho.
To understand, you have to go back to when they found him.
It was thick with woods where he lived.
It seems that it was in a gully where they found him.
In a gully! He was lying on the ground with seven women.
They were all Hiawatha's daughters and they were dead.
It says they found seven girls lying there.
I don't know if they took him or what, but he had his "thing" over his shoulder.
Maybe that's what killed them.
His "thing" was so long he had it over his shoulder.
He must have used it like a club for it to have killed those women.

The word Tadodaho means in translation, "Snakes Entangled."
When they first found him his hair was all messed up.
It looked like snakes coming out of there.
That's what the Peacemaker saw

and felt with all those snakes that the Tadodaho must be evil.
He was so evil!
All of the people were afraid of Tadodaho
because he was so mean and evil.
He was the most feared one of all
even though the other leaders were all feared by the people, too.
The Peacemaker looked for the evil ones.
The Peacemaker knew that if they were reformed
they would make good leaders.
His mission on Earth was to reform them
for the good of the people.
Once he found them, they weren't evil when he left them.
They were gentle then.
When the Peacemaker reformed the leaders,
even the Tadodaho, he gave them the Instructions.
That was the beginning of the Five Nations Confederacy.
It became Six Nations when the Tuscarora joined
after being pushed out of what is now North Carolina.
Because the Peacemaker changed the original Tadodaho
to start working for the benefit of his people,
after he died, the people used his name
as the title of the highest position in the Confederacy.
Nobody knows how many leaders have held the position of Tadodaho.
It's talked in the Longhouse that there have been
over fifty in the last one thousand years.
Once selected, you hold the office for life
unless you start working for yourself and not the people.
The chiefs can remove you for that.
Since I became Tadodaho in 1969
I have done my best and worked for only the good.

But I didn't think about being the Tadadoho or even a chief
when I was young. Even as a young man
my mother started to get scared that I was not going to get married.
I just didn't feel like settling down.

That was the word, I didn't want to settle down yet.
I didn't want to get tied up. I wanted to play the fields.
It's true there's no other feeling like sex.
That's why it means so much. It revives your sensations
and it brings back that youthful spirit.
If you're weak, it can make a mockery out of you.
It's so strong and it's so good, that it's hard to fight it.
You've got to be pretty strong to fight it,
even though it's in everybody's urge, every human being.
I had an old friend who wanted me to have sex with her.
My girl friend that I went to school with growing up;
we liked each other. I was really crazy over her.
Sometimes girls like you, maybe love you,
but they don't really show it. Then, there are some that are bored
and they will come on to you.
I've had that happen, too.
Some almost forced me to kiss them.
I've had some that backed me up against the wall.
They wanted to kiss me and I didn't want to.
I was kinda afraid.

Sex is good.
It has such a strong pull that it can cloud your vision.
It's one of the stronger powers that were put here on Mother Earth.
But if all you think about is sex,
then you're not going to be doing your ceremony.
Give that sex power only the attention it deserves and no more.
That way you won't miss out on all the rest of the things
the Creator has for you.
Train your mind.
You can do it if you don't let your body lead you.

The teachings of the Longhouse prepared me
to be able to withstand the temptation.
I give all the credit to my spiritual teachings.
Some would say that I'm nuts for passing it up.

Even at my age the urge is still there.
It has lessened, but not too much.
The urge is there.

I didn't ask to be Tadodaho.
I never planned in my mind to one day become Tadodaho.
People did it, but it was the Creator's plan for me.
That's the way it is with all the chiefs and faithkeepers,
the clan mothers, and the clans. The Creator has His plan.
There's the circle and there's a place prepared by the Creator
for everyone in the circle.

It's that way with all the people on the Earth.
That's why it's important
everyone walks on the path back to the Creator,
because He has things planned for us while we're here.
That's why every morning when I wake up I'm ready for the day.
I don't know what's coming, but I know
the Creator has something for me.
He may even bring a trip my way
and I'll be traveling somewhere.
But if we're off His path,
we may miss out on what He's got planned for us.

My path is nobody else's.
You have your path.
Everybody has a path.
You're on it whether you know it or not.
At some time everybody must realize it.
Maybe some don't. But everybody's path leads back to the Creator.
To be able to see the Creator on the other side,
you make sure you find your path in this life.
If you don't, then the Creator has more lessons for you.
That means you didn't learn what you were supposed to in this life,
so you need more experiences.
It's better you find and follow your path now.

You know you're on your path because
you become happy.
It's like being contented or comfortable.
That doesn't mean you just sit around.
It's the opposite.
You know what you're supposed to be doing
and you're doing it. You're busy about your divine work.
We all have things we are to be doing
for the Creator and creation.
Being on your path means you're about that work.

Steve Wall 9

It's a good feeling.
Nobody can tell you if you're on your path.
You just know it inside. When you are ready,
things come to you that pull you in a certain direction.
That's your path telling you that you're on it.
Doing those things means you're following the path.
It's a good feeling.

If you are looking for people to praise you,
you're not paying attention to where you're going.
Looking to others is a sign that you're not working for the creation.
That's a sure way to lose your way and get off your path.
It's easier to stay on it than figure out how to get back on it.

I've heard it both ways. You only live once
and that this is not the only time you've been here.
Sometimes I think it's hard to get it right just living once.
So maybe we have lived before.
I think I've done better this time
if there ever was another me that lived in the past.
I sure hope that sooner or later I do get it right,
otherwise I'm wasting the Creator's time.
I'm glad He's got a lot of patience. He's needed it for me.
Maybe I've used up all His patience and there's no more for you.
That means you better get on your path fast so you won't need it.

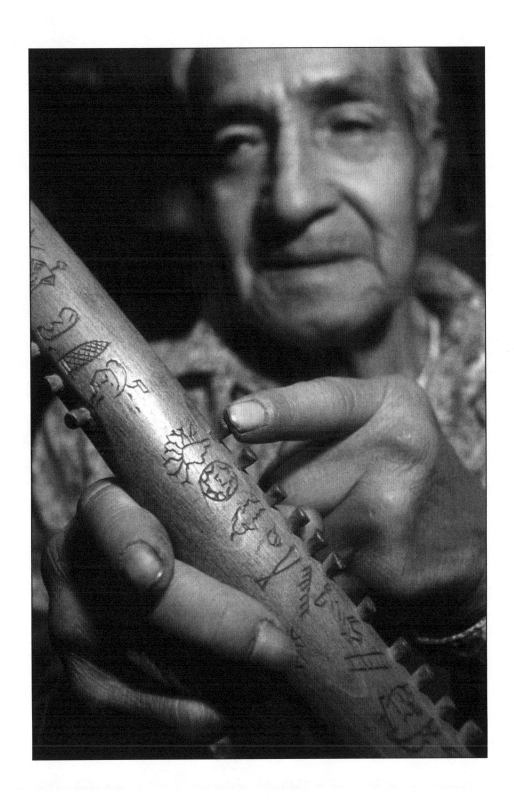

"Watch what you say,
somebody is always listening"

Listening to
Instructions

There must be laughter.
That's one of our Instructions.
When the Peacemaker was leaving us
to go back to the Creator,
he told us to have laughter.
That would show him how much
we were enjoying being here on the earth
and being a part of the creation.
When times are the toughest
we're supposed to have laughter.

It helps us get through the hard parts that come our way.
When the people have decisions to make
and things get tense between them,
laughter breaks that tenseness.
Somebody will tell a joke to make everyone laugh,
then they can go back to making the decision without being angry.
We're not supposed to take everything in too serious a way.
We're always to have the Good Mind. If our mind is clouded,
how can good decisions be made? Laughter clears our mind
and reminds us of the Creator.
So, that's why he instructed us to always have laughter.
Some people don't think Indians laugh.
That shows they haven't been around Indians.
I just tell them that we're still following our Instructions.
That means we still laugh.

Mostly I hear.
You can learn a lot more when you're listening
than when you're talking.
I never knew anybody who learned anything by talking.
Until you start listening
you'll never have too much to talk about
because you never learned anything.
If you don't know anything,
it won't be too long
before there will be nobody listening
to what you have to say. So, it's better
to sit and listen instead of talking.
People will start paying attention to you,
if you're just sitting. They will be wondering
what's going through your mind. Then,
when you speak up, they'll all be listening.
Somebody who's always talking
soon shows what he knows.
Usually it's not much. His head is empty.
He never stopped long enough

to fill it with anything of value
for the good of the people.

The Creator made us for honoring Him.
He put in us the ability to work for the good of all.
One of the things He did
was give us ears, and ears are not mouths.
Ears were put on the side of our heads
so that we would hear all that goes on around us.
That's to let us know things before we talk.
Our mouths are on the front of our face
so that our words can be directed.
We're to use that gift of speech for specific purposes.
It should be limited, otherwise we can mislead.
When we mislead, we can influence the people
to take a wrong direction or course of action.
That can cause a lot of harm.
People would start "running in the woods."
That's how we describe people who forget the Creator.
We say "they're running in the woods."
When that happens people will personally suffer
and even turn on each other.

Watch what you say. Somebody is always listening.
It could be another human being
and that person could turn your words around on you,
especially if you talk about somebody.
It's not just human beings who may hear you.
Spirits are always about, and they hear you, too.
There are people who can call on the spirits
and the spirits will tell them things.

They can even tell on you. That can be very dangerous.
Nothing is said or done in secret

because there is always at least one who is listening.
You want what you say to be good,
that way you never have to explain
or try to cover up anything.
You never have to apologize. People will learn
they can trust you to always be truthful in your words.
They will give you respect for that, because they will know
that you would never say anything in a harmful way.
Even in your language the Creator will be pleased with you,
and your words will never come back to harm you.
You know you can hurt yourself
by the way you talk about others. Be good to yourself
while you're being good to other people.

I never call on the Creator for anything.
I don't have to. Nobody else does either.
The Creator gives us all we need in this life.
He gave us a good mind to think clearly.
He instructed Mother Earth
to provide all the necessities to sustain our lives.
She's still doing that.
She's doing her duty.
She gives us our food and she replenishes the waters.
She causes the plants to grow for our medicines.
So our lives are taken care of.

I study the stars. They talk to me.
They tell me when it's time to do things.
Sometimes they tell me what's going to happen.
There are times I don't want to know
because that places a lot of responsibility on me
to warn the people. It's troubling
when nobody wants to make the changes
necessary to stop certain things from happening.
You can do that. You can prevent things from taking place
if enough people will take action. If they don't

then I know what's coming.
I do what I can and sometimes it's not enough.
Then there are times the people do take action
and whatever was going to happen doesn't
because of them. That's when I am relieved.
No matter what, I have to do my duty.
That's all the Creator asks all of us to do.

It's tough knowing things.
That's what my elders would say.
I know their meaning now.
It's like watching the video, only it's in my head.
I can see the up-coming leaders and the singers.
I see the trades they'll take and the arts in every one of them.
The toughest part is knowing which ones will probably go over the hill.
It fills my heart up and makes me work harder
for the children who are coming behind me.
That's why you've got to go gentle with them.
A kindness can help to turn them toward the Creator.

Some people think life is so hard.
I know about that.
I've worked hard myself,
but I never paid much attention to material things.
If I had them I wouldn't know what to do with them.
It's not something that ever interested me.
I rather think about how good life is.
I've enjoyed being here on Mother Earth.
I want to stay just as long as the Creator allows me to live.
It's so wonderful to smell the breeze
when winter starts to turn toward spring
and the wind shifts from the south.
Oh, what a good feeling!
And you know that you made it through the winter
and you're thankful. It made you tougher, you're stronger for it.
Each season is good. Mother Earth is working for you.

She's doing her duty. It's a good feeling
to be alive and see the changes in nature.
There are so many good people,
and if you're alive that means
you're going to get to meet some more of them.
There are so many places to go.
The world is so big, so many cultures to visit.
If you're alive, you may get to travel and get to know them.
That is a hope that gives you a good feeling.

Once I got a glimpse of what it'll be like
on the other side with the Creator.
I was up at Six Nations Reserve in Canada.
It was a hot day and kinda breezy a little bit,
but it was nice in the shade.
I looked out over this field, looked like a wheat field.
You knew there was a breeze,
because the wind made the wheat move back and forth.
Made me think of water.
You could even see the waves
when the wind was hitting the top and moving the grass.
It reminded me that that's just the way it looked
just before you get to heaven . . .
on your way to the Creator's place.
You could see the waves in the field.

I'm not afraid of dying. When I do,
I know I will get to where the Creator is.
But I like it here. It's a good place to be.
Some time along your path
you realize that you don't have to worry about anything.
You know you made it this far
and the Creator will be with you as you follow your trail.
When you come to know this, you have peace inside yourself.
That's when you really start to live. It's exciting

because you know there's a tomorrow
filled with new things to experience.
Living is good. Death is to go to the Creator,
so you can look forward to that,
but being on Mother Earth is so good.
If I had a choice I'd never leave her.
While I'm here I'm going to make the best of the time I have.
When it's my time to go to the other world,
I don't think I'm going to go easy.
This is where I want to be.

Steve Wall 19

"The thing wrong with the world is that people don't have their Instructions."

Return

This is the time people are starting to return home.
Indians are doing it. They left to get away,
but they never could get their land out of their mind.
Now they are coming back.

Indians are not the only ones.
Others want to know where they came from.
They feel an emptiness and now they are searching.

Everybody is originally from some place.
They want to know who their family was from a long time ago.
Then they want to know about what country they lived in.
Most times it was in Europe; that's where the colonists came from.
After that, they want to learn about their old traditions.
They're not satisfied with just knowing about traditions here.
Those are all made up so you'll buy things,
and there's no deep meaning to them.
Like I said, they're searching and that's one path.

What you call the United States,
we Indians call the Great Turtle Island.
This is where the Creator planted us
and when He did, He made us free.
Europeans were not planted here,
but you came here because you wanted to be free like us.
In our original Instructions we were told that nobody owned the land
except the Creator. That's why we welcomed you.
But Europeans claimed the land they lived on was theirs.
That was funny to our people because we knew
that nobody could own the land.
Then the Europeans decided
that all of Great Turtle Island was theirs to own.
That wasn't funny to us anymore.

Our people were made up of nations then
and we still are. We are sovereign, every one of the nations.
That means that we are free to live as we have always done.
Nobody can tell us what to do.
When they made the Great Turtle Island the United States,

they studied our way of life and copied it.
We call our gathering of chiefs the Grand Council.
That's what Benjamin Franklin wanted to call yours.
But that didn't win out, you named your government the Congress.
Then, they told us that we had to do what the government told us to do.
The United States government made treaties with us,
but started breaking them right away.
Because we were sovereign nations we had to start fighting
for the land that the Creator said
was where we were supposed to live.

A lot of our people died
trying to say that nobody could own the land
and more died trying to say that the government couldn't tell us what to do.
We are still trying to say the same thing.
We are free, but the children of the Europeans
are learning that they are not free.
The government can tell them what they have to do
and how they have to live.

The United States government will take everything from you
and leave you on the street.
The government is not looking out for your welfare.
You can see that in the end it's not going to turn out right,
but the people don't see it.
We are all visitors here. We're only visiting this earth.
We're all going to come and go continuously.
We're not here forever.
So we make the best of it while we're here visiting.
So why are you paying while you're visiting?

What if I went to your place to visit
and I had to pay you?
Would that be right?

Well, that is the way that government is working on the people.
It's going to cost the people a lot of money as you go,
but where is it going?
Somebody is getting it.
I can tell you that those getting it can't take it with them.
Those leaders that are millionaires
came to be millionaires while they were supposed to be serving the people.
This is heaven to them. So this is the only place they'll ever have it.
I'm not going to make it to the Creator's place
by making a living off the people.
Those who do will never get to the Creator's place.
When you steal land that is for everybody,
you're going against the wishes of the Creator.

        We are all sovereign people.
        You, too! Down to the last person.
        Us Indians are still fighting to stay free
        like the Creator made us. When will you?
        Someday you'll learn
        that only the Creator can take the land
        the Creator gave for everybody.
        Until then we'll all be suffering.
        It's one thing we'll all be doing together.

The thing wrong with the world
is that people don't have instructions.
We were told almost three hundred years ago
that people would be coming to us and asking for our instructions.
We were told back in the 1700s
that there'd be a day when white people would be coming to us,
asking for instructions and finding out the way we think.

        Indians joke that when they see a white man coming,
        they see a question mark walking down the road.

That's not one of the things I laugh about.
I feel for the ones who feel lost.
I tell them to use common sense and learn to listen.
The Creator has the answers.
A lot of people are searching for what they don't have.
They're searching for what they don't get in an education.
They're searching for the wisdom of a whole way of life.
So they come to the Indians.
That's why I say it's in the prophecies
that they are coming to us,
because they are wanting to learn our way of life,
what it is all about.
It's true, I get a lot of people, even college people,
who want to know how to be a "Human Being."
We don't laugh at the white people.
Most of the Indians can't laugh
because even they haven't been brought up
in the Longhouse like I have.
They've got to learn too. Even some of the chiefs have had to learn
and I don't know how much they have learned.

There are many abilities that come from the Creator.
We have some who can talk to the spirit world.
We used to have some who dreamed
and saw things that could help the people.
Others studied the stars.
They told us when to plant,
when to have ceremonies,
what the weather was going to be
and what was coming.
Some knew how to interpret the messages
that came to us when we returned from seeking our vision.
Then there were medicine people
who knew the plants and herbs.
They could even talk to them
and the plants would tell them what each one was good for.

Also, the medicine men and women knew
how to prepare the different medicines for the illnesses.

Now there are only a few who can do any of those things.
Who can even talk to the plants anymore!
So much is being lost and our people are suffering because of that.
Only a few understand why the ceremonies are so important.
Carrying them on shows the Creator we are giving Him thanks.
That pleases Him, so He allows the world
to continue on a while longer.
If we don't keep up the ceremonies then Mother Earth will start to weep.
She will be sad
and the people will no longer be able to hear
who they are and what their abilities are.
That's when the people will suffer.
I think the beginning of suffering is close on us.

I learned what I know in the Longhouse.
That was my school. The elders were my teachers.
Your schools don't teach you those things.
There's coming a day when your education will fail you
because they don't teach you the spirituality.
You learn how to get a job, make money, and manage business,
but you don't know about the Creator's place
or about what your path is.
You don't learn about the ceremonies or the witnesses.
You can't go to your churches
because there are so many different ones
you don't know which one is the right one.
The Creator's brother jumbled them up into confusion.

What can you use education for
when there's nothing that will work?
Everything'll be coming down

and there'll be a time when money will be of no use.
Why work when you can't buy food?
The people will be coming back and planting.
That's what I'm seeing.
It's getting nearer and nearer, and I can't say when.
But as the years go on,
you can tell that the people have started coming back.
All the people will be coming home.
They will be coming to power again.
Must be something going on out there
when they want to come back.

People ask me to come and speak.
They want to know about the spiritual and spirituality.
They question me about what our beliefs are.
I have to tell everybody
that He has sent His message down to us to follow His Instructions.
That will lead you back to him.

You come to us asking questions,
but we tell you things you don't understand.
Our ceremonies come from the Original Instructions
that were given to us
and we've kept them going from the beginning.
You were given Instructions, too,
but your leaders hid them so they could control you.
If you started doing our ceremonies
you could get into trouble
and stir up things that you wouldn't know how to handle.
It would be like letting something out of a box that could hurt you.
You've got to know what you're doing
when you do things like talk to the spirits.
They can help you and they can hurt you.
You don't want to do ceremonies unless you understand them.
I say you have to have the education that won't fail you.

All you can do is start planting again
and it will come to you as you go along.
That's the first step of your path back to the Creator.

We can change things if we pay attention
to how we live and treat others. All we've got to do
is show respect. People are so afraid now.
The way of life they were taught
turned out to be different.
It's like they were taken in with a lie.
Not everyone got rich or had a big house and fine cars.
They gave everything they had
to a company or a corporation
and then they found out they didn't have a job.
Now everybody is trying to take care of themselves
because everything around them fell apart.
Nobody knows where to turn. So people are angry
and look only to take care of themselves.

What we have to do is make the system accountable
and make it change. It is important
that everybody gives up being so selfish.
When we share the things we have with others,
then everybody will be taken care of.
You can't take care of yourself if you're taking from others.
It will come back on you. The more bad you give out,
the more you get. If you give good, you get good
because it's all a circle. Sometimes we miss how simple it is.
One day we will get the message.
It's better we use our minds and sort it out for ourselves
before it's done for us by the Creator.
If we continue as we're going,
we'll destroy ourselves.
The Creator will step to one side and let us do it to ourselves.

Like I said, we can change that.
Follow The Instructions and live in peace.

It's hard to do the ceremonies
when you are angry or fighting with other people.
It is better to forgive
because how can you give thanks
when you are filled with anger?
You can't think about the goodness of the Creator
if your mind is off in another direction that controls you.
Let the Creator take care of those things that you can't.
Don't get tangled up in things that are not of your doing.
They will hang you. Just untangle your own mess
and separate yourself from the trouble
somebody else brought on themselves.
They'll be answering for their actions
and you'll be happy going on your own way.

A lot of people have lost their way,
but they still kinda believe in what they were taught.
Even some of my people at home have lost their way
but they come to me in times of trouble.
People want to know who our medicine men and women are.
They call them the holy ones.
We are all holy and so are you.
We are all the Creator's people.
We still have our ceremonies to honor the Creator.
You once had yours, too.
I tell everybody who asks as much as I know.
I say they can find their ceremony if they use the good mind.
The Creator still speaks to every people on Mother Earth.
He'll speak to you. You've got to listen.
You can't hear from just reading or watching television.
You have to return to your circle. That will be hard
because your ancestors covered your circle with confusion.
Clear that away and there will be your ceremony.

"I myself have no power. It's the people behind me
who give me any power that I have.
Real power comes only from the Creator.
If you're asking about strength, then I can say
that the greatest strength is gentleness."

Indigenous people of the earth are strong.
We Indian people are the original people of this continent.
We call it Great Turtle Island, and we're indigenous to this land.
We are strong, too. We've had to be just to survive.
You can see that we're still here. We'll be here
long after the Europeans are gone
because they are destroying the land.
They can stop what they're doing.
I hope they do and make this place better for everyone.
There's enough land for everybody.

Being Strong

And there's enough money to make sure
that nobody is hungry and that everybody has a home.
But that will be hard to accomplish
because of all the greed.
Greed is destroying what is sacred to us.
It must become sacred for all human beings
because this land is what sustains all of life.

Yes, we are strong. All survivors are. They have to be.
But what has happened is
that many of my people have behaved like children,
running around in all directions,
raising their voices just to hear themselves
because of all the abuse.
Sometimes the people turn on each other,
take life and hurt their families
and other people's families. Some took up with drugs,
and alcohol has weakened many ones.
Now is the time for everybody to honor the Creator
and honor themselves
by remembering their ceremonies
and taking care of their bodies.
They must listen to the good voice inside of themselves
and join together with one voice by using the good mind.
The drugs must be put aside.
Nobody should keep taking in the alcohol.
Bad spirits take over when those things are used.
Everybody must bury all the hatred
for what the Europeans
and big corporations
and politicians have been doing.

We're doing our best,
but sometimes we're fighting the whole world.
We're trying to keep the world going a little longer.

Everything around us is trying to destroy us
by getting us to forget our language and our way of life.
That's why we are fighting over our land.
A long time ago the government
and the church people
tried to get us to get an education
and make us forget what land meant to us.
They thought that if we forgot,
we'd move to the cities and become like white people.
Then, we'd not be recognized as Indians.
I guess they figured we'd die away.
But we didn't go away. We're still here.
We still know what Mother Earth means to us
and our languages are still spoken by many.
We will continue with our ceremonies.

Now we must join with the indigenous peoples
around the world and become one
with respect for all of life. We can do this
by showing that we are stronger
than all the forces that have tried to separate
and remove us from Mother Earth.
Everybody needs to know that life is sacred
and we are staying put. We will not be angry but determined.
We will not be ruled by our own hatred.
Nothing will make us be filled with fear.
The politicians have no power over us.
The corporations don't have power either;
not even the government.

We're taught that you've got to have skin seven layers thick.
You have to develop it. It's a discipline to do that.
There's work to it. But when your skin is thick
nobody can get at you. They can't touch you.
They can't hurt your feelings or cause you to have jealousy.

Steve Wall 33

Money won't tempt you.
If somebody works bad medicine on you,
it'll never find your weakness.
It'll go right back on that person who sent it your way.
That's why we say you've got to have skin seven layers thick.
If something touches you a little,
you'll always have another layer of skin for protection.

Before we can come to this place,
we must respect each other. To do that,
every "Human Being" must use their good mind
and not be taken in by the evil one
who works on those who are weaker
and swayed by greed and hatred.
We must know we are strong.

That goes for nonindigenous people, too.
Even Americans are indigenous to some land.
Those who listen to the evil one are swayed, too.
They're not weak, they have been victims, too.

Now we all must join together and know how strong we are.
The Creator promised that
if we followed The Instructions
then He would take care of us. He has proved that
because the people are still here.
Mother Earth is still doing her duty, too.
So we are still here
and our children will be following us.
Nobody can stop the generations.
The important issue is how will we live.
Will we live in fear and do as the authorities tell us
and give us nothing in return? Or will we be strong enough
to unite for the good of everybody?
I say we will!
We are now coming together
with all our brothers and sisters all over the world.
You may not be seeing it yet, but it is happening.
None of us are going to be victims anymore.

"I'm working for the Creation.
I refuse to take part
in its destruction."

Becoming Human

The Creator gave us our name Haudenosaunee.
That means "Human Beings," not Indian.
There's no such thing as Indian,
just "Human Being."
If we were Indian, we'd be from India.
We're "Human Beings."

The Creator planted us here.
He planted lots of things.
So our duty is to keep thanking the Creator.
When we pray it's a greeting. We don't ask for anything.
Church people ask for things in their prayers.
We don't. We greet Him by thanking Him
for all the things He has left for "Human Beings" to survive.

There is no reason to ask.
He has given us everything for us to enjoy.
That's why our greeting is thanks.
That's why we have to thank Him for all He left here.
We give thanks for all kinds of medicine,
the berries, water, the air, and the land.
To show this appreciation to the Creator
we have ceremony.
We must show our appreciation for what He has given us
because without the earth we wouldn't survive.

Doing the ceremonies means you're giving thanks,
and we have no choice about it.
Sooner or later we all will remember
to do the duties we were instructed to do.
Sooner is better.
Later brings the suffering
that will cause us to remember the Creator.
The decision as to when it will be
is always up to each person.
In the end everybody will be doing the same thing,
and that is remembering.

I'm going to always be following The Instructions now.
You can wait to give thanks, if you want to.
Not me! I know the pain that waiting causes.

Nobody knows what specific suffering
someone will have to go through
that will bring them back to the remembering.
I'll just live each day in thanksgiving.
You do whatever and however you want.
It's your life . . . and maybe that of your loved ones.
You just never know. I'll promise you that I'll do my best
to give thanks and carry on the ceremonies
for all the people of the world
for as long as I live.
As long as one person is doing that,
maybe the suffering will be postponed
for a while. But it's coming. Still I'll keep trying
as long as I have the ability to do it.
After that, I don't know.
I hope others will get the message before that time.
The Creator hears the prayers of even one person,
but there must be at least one. It's better if there's a lot,
but I hope there's always at least one.
One can be a powerful force.
Even one pleases the Creator.
It shows the Creator that somebody is paying attention.

In the beginning everything was spoken, even messages from the Creator.
There was no writing.
But we were told that we're all visitors here on earth.
When we die we'll all go back to Mother Earth.
That's why the Creator gave Instructions
how to get back up to where He is.
He wants us to get back, but the evil one says, "No."
He's working pretty hard to control us
so we won't get back up there.
Evil is always working against good.
If you're weak, he has you,
but you can be strong by listening to the Creator's Instructions.
You just have to use common sense.

Another Instruction is to give thanks to Mother Earth, as well.
Giving thanks is to give honor
and to honor is to show respect.
Doing that means you're becoming a "Human Being."
The more you become a "Human Being"
the more you remember your ceremonies.
All the people on Mother Earth
were given their ceremonies. Carrying them on
is one of the duties of "Human Beings."

The Creator made everything equal.
"Human Beings" are the same to the Creator
as every other living thing.
But He gave "Human Beings" the responsibility
to watch out for the rest of His creation.
That makes us the guardians.
Look what we've done.
Instead of being the guardians,
some people have learned how to destroy
because of greed.
The animals and fish and the birds don't do that;
they just go on with their duties.
So we've got to help change people's minds
so that they will protect the land,
so that their seventh generation from now
will have some place to live.

Only people know good and bad.
Animals and birds know only the good.
They know their duties and do them.
They don't even question.
They don't have to spend time thinking about it.
There's nothing for them to worry about,
the Creator promised to take care of them.

The Instructions say that men and women are equal, too.
They've got to learn that one is not above the other.
It takes both to create the children who are coming from behind us.

The woman is like Mother Earth. She brings life.
If you hurt her, you are going against the Creator and cutting life down.
You have to have man and woman for children to come into the world.
But the woman knows how to take care of the life of the children.
Man doesn't know as much;
he doesn't pay attention to how to help them grow and learn.
The woman understands things that the man never learned.
She can make decisions on what is best for the welfare of everybody.
Men are too easy to rush into things, like war.
The woman can think things out
in a slower more thoughtful manner
because she is closer to Mother Earth.

Sometimes the woman can get off her path, too.
But when she follows The Instructions
that were put into her by the Creator
and is handed down through our way,
then everybody benefits.
Without the woman there'd be no life.
The man should never try to control the woman
or the woman control the man.
To have harmony both of them should work together.

We have to take care of the children.
The Creator gave us that duty.
Everybody is responsible for them.
They are not supposed to suffer.
If even one child in the world is going hungry,
we're supposed to feed them.
If any one of the children is going without clothes

or has no place to sleep
or is not looked after,
we're not doing what the Creator told us to do.
All the children are important.
One is not more important than another
no matter where they live in the world.
Someday the ones who live long enough to grow up will take over.
It's better that they use the good mind
in making the decisions for the coming generations.
If they weren't taken care of, how can they do that?

I've always paid attention to little kids.
When I was younger and I'd see a young kid
who wanted to get back to his house but he was afraid,
I'd go take him back.
The other guys wouldn't do it.
They said I was chicken hearted, because I was helping other people.
My heart talked to me. Some call it tenderhearted.
I couldn't stand to see a kid suffer. I felt their feelings.
So I go out of my way and help them.

The elders know about all the children.
They could always see how the children would turn out.
That's why they would help to guide the children
in the right direction.
Some would become singers of the sacred songs.
Others would be faithkeepers.
They knew the trades they'd be best at.
They could see the artist in each one.
Then, the elders could see
which ones would be strong in the Longhouse
and the ones who would "go over the hill"
to get away from their teachings.
Now that I'm older I can see what my elders saw.
I guess you've got to get old before it comes to you.

Every one of us has been a child once.
Some continue to be like a child.
It is okay to be a child when you are little and on up to teenager.
But the time comes when we must grow to be a "Human Being."
You get to act like a child when you're a child.
That is the way life is supposed to be. The Creator made it that way
so we could make mistakes, learn lots of lessons,
and get an education with experiences.
We don't accuse children of being children,
but even in those years they must have teachers
to show them how to discipline themselves
without being harmful to their lives or bodies.
Then we are supposed to grow up and become full "Human Beings."
We have to account. When we understand, we answer to the Creator
and not to anybody else on earth, then we turn ourselves around
and find the path the Creator made for each and every "Human Being."

The Creator is not a he or a she. It's just the Creator.
Sometimes I say He, but the Creator's not either.
The Creator is both and neither.
It's hard to understand, but it's so simple.
Simple things confuse most people but not "Human Beings."
"Human Beings" are more than just people.
Being a "Human Being" is being close to the Creator.
When a "Human Being" is close to the Creator,
then they just know things. It's called "the knowing."
"Human Beings" don't know all things.
Each one is given a different ability.
Some know some things. Others know other things.
But no one knows it all. That's why we need each other.
When we come together we can know more things.
That's what participating in the ceremonies is all about.
When we are together in the circle, we are one.
As one we can be more in "the knowing."
In the circle we get closer to the Creator
and those different abilities unite for the good of us all.

That's when everything becomes possible.
We know that nothing is impossible with the Creator.
The Creator gave us His abilities
and He spread them around among us.
That was so that each one of us would use our ability for good.

But He also wanted us to realize
that we had to come together in the circle
so that we could sense just how powerful the Creator is.
When we're in that circle and living with it in our hearts everyday,
great things happen that can't easily be explained.
He gave us the circle so that we can benefit from being one with Him
and one with each other.

We are all teachers. None of us asked for the job.
Maybe some did, and if they did,
they didn't know what they were asking for.
Anyway, whether some asked for it and the rest of us didn't,
we're all teachers.
Somebody is always watching.
That person will follow in your path for awhile.
Our lives should always be lived in a way
that you would want that person to live.
If you don't live it right, that person won't either.
So you can't blame anybody for what they do
if you weren't a good teacher. Follow the Creator's way
and you'll always be a good teacher
whether you know you're one or not.
You are! Take my word for it.
Maybe you think nobody's watching
and you don't have to be a good teacher.
It's better you don't ask if anybody's watching.
That way you'll not be disappointed
if nobody's paying you any attention. It's best to just go on
and act like you're being watched if it makes you feel any better.

There's got to be something about you that's worth watching.
But the important thing is that however you live your life,
it's between you and the Creator.

I don't want to just be thinking about whether anybody is watching me or not.
I want to be living in a way that the Creator will be happy with me.

"There's nothing hidden.
There are always witnesses around,
both good and bad spirits."

Spirits

The dead can hurt you. They're the ones
who did not find their way to the Creator
because of the way they lived.
They can be up to no good because they're so unhappy.
They were even that way when they were alive.
It's no different when they pass away.
It's very important that you live upright.

When you do
there is nothing that can be used against you
by the people who can talk to the spirits.
Some who call on the spirits do it for good reasons
and talk only to the good spirits who reside with the Creator.
But there are the restless spirits, too.
Those are the ones who are out for no good.
People who want to deal with bad medicine
are the ones who call on the restless spirits.
They look for things you do
so that they can touch you and bring you down.
It is important that you live above such things.
Live an honorable life and keep your path clean.
Then nothing you do can hurt you.
You can't be touched by the practices of those kind of people.
You won't ever have to account for your deeds
and you will never have anything to fear.
Fear is the way those people get in.
If you have no fear, you are free.

When a spiritual reader talks to the spirits,
the spirits tell her about their memories.
They say what happened and what they saw.
If she asks them to go somewhere and check on somebody,
they come back and tell her what was going on.
Remember what I told you. There's always a witness.
Spirits don't take money or cars or houses with them when they die,
but they do take the thoughts of the living.

Sometimes you may do things at night
that you think you're hiding; well you're not.
There are spirits that wander. They come at night
and go back to the spiritual world the next morning.
There's always a witness. Witnesses can talk.
There's no such thing as doing something alone.

Right now the spirits are watching.
You don't know they're around, but they are.

I'll tell you an example.
Vince Johnson was at my mother's wake.
Well, that night during the wake
everyone was going out of the Longhouse
to go get something to eat.
He said, "Well, I'll stay."
In our custom somebody's got to stay with the dead person.
So while he was there alone walking around,
he looked out through the window.
Because it was dark out, he couldn't see anything.
Well, what do the lights do on the window at night?
They reflect back what's inside. So,
when he looked out the window,
he saw that reflection.
There were people sitting on the benches in the Longhouse.
There were women sitting in there
with their shawls over their heads
and they were having a wake. They were there
but all the people had left.
But he saw those people in the reflection.
When he turned around from the window and looked,
there was nobody there. He was sure then
that they were dead people who came back.
He understood what was happening;
we know that the spirits come back.

When the body's dead, well the spirit's right there.
That's why our speakers say to the spirit
that we're trying to do everything to their liking.
We try to appease them.
When we cook the food, we don't use salt.
When we fill the plates with food,

we set one aside for the dead.
We put it on the coffin.
We never leave the body alone because the spirit's there.
They're around for ten days
after we put the body in the ground,
then we have one big last meal.
On the tenth day there's the big feast, then they leave.
Our way tells us that people that passed away
can help you and they can harm you.
We feed them so they won't harm us.
Then we give all their things away on the tenth day.
We give everything away
so the spirit won't be back looking for them.
The family is allowed to keep one thing that they valued
so they can look at it
and be reminded of the one that passed away.
You give their things away to their friends as a reminder of them.
The spirits are watching.
They hear you.
They watch and they listen to everything you say.
You only select those to stay with the body during the wake who want to.
The dead don't want to be left alone.

    When there's a wake,
    you're never supposed to go out into the night alone.
    See, there are two levels in the spiritual world.
    One level goes to the Creator and the other one doesn't make it.

There are both good and bad spirits there at the same time.
Good spirits are protectors
while the others are trying to hurt you.
The bad spirits come back every day
late in the afternoon
and they leave early in the morning.
That's why I say there's always a witness around.

They're witnessing things.
When you think you're alone doing things,
that nobody sees you,
well, the spirits do.

For example, I helped the police one time
find a kid that had been killed.
I went to a reader at Six Nations Reserve in Canada,
and she talked to the dead.
The dead told her where the kid was.
She talked to the spirit.
There's nothing hidden.

Those spirits who didn't go on to the Creator are around.
Those who don't follow the good
learn that these spirits are ready to do mischief.
A few dedicate themselves to working with those spirits
and directing them towards people
so they can influence their minds.
It's hate and greed that makes them do it.
You have to pay them to work the spirits
depending on the way you want them to cause harm.
To do that you have to get their attention.
Certain kinds of medicine bring them.
You use the medicine to reach them.
I don't want to touch that,
so I guess I'll never find out how the spirits are hired.
But when the dark spirits are around I know it.
I can't really explain it. It's something I sense.
There's a pressure I feel.
It's not a good feeling, like a dark cloud and it makes me uneasy.

People that work bad medicine do it on their own people.
They do it to make money.

Some people go to those kind of people who do it
to get back at somebody they think has hurt them.
So they use the dead people, the bad spirit.
They hire that spirit in their own family.
That spirit is one that never made it to the Creator.
Those that didn't make it are hungry
and that's why they're willing to do the evil.
It's all a false power, though,
and it will come back on everyone involved.
Evil is out to harm you, not to help.
So the only power in it is the power to hurt.
I'm only studying medicine that's good and helps people.
I stay away from the other. I don't touch it.

When you die, you make a trip back
to all those people you met in this life
and return to all those places you visited.
That's what you do before you go on to the Creator.
If you lived a good life, you just say your good-byes.
If there were problems between you and somebody else,
you try to apologize and ask for forgiveness.
I've met a lot of people and gone a lot of places,
so I've got a long journey to make once I die.
I'll just be saying my good-byes on my trip.
I'll partly be sad, because I know
I'm not going to want to be going on that trip.
I'd rather be staying,
but I'll be looking forward to visiting with all those I've met.
I'll enjoy going back to all those places around the world I have visited.

In the spring we have the memorial for all the dead.
That's when we remember all of them
and we invite them in and feed them
and invite them to dance.
If we didn't feed them they could harm us.

We do it early in the spring
because all living things are asleep.
Later in the spring everything comes back to life.
The dead have just gone on into the spiritual world.
In our way, it says they've gone on ahead.
When you die you go on ahead.
That's why there's no good-bye in our language.
There's always the circle of birth and death and rebirth.
It's kinda hard to explain.

Everything in time will go back to dirt.
It says that we all are made from Mother Earth
and we will go back to Mother Earth.
But the spirit goes on.
Our spirit is not buried,
but sticks around for ten days and then it goes.
There are ceremonies that are done
so the bad luck won't go to the people around there.
When you dig up graves and expose the bones to the air,
it is bad luck.
Once the body goes that way, it stays with the Mother Earth.

The spirits are there and seeing what is happening to their bodies.
The spirit gets stirred up.
I've had to burn tobacco to try and talk to them, to reach them.
It's like sending a message to the Creator.
It is the tobacco that makes the message reach the Creator.
It's like an antennae so I can reach the spirits to talk to them.
It is to calm them, and they have to have food in the end to satisfy them.

The spirits are concerned.
They know their bones are down there.
They are very much alive, like a human being,
but they're into another world, the spiritual world.

Steve Wall 53

54　To Become a Human Being

When I've had to rebury the bones
after they've been dug up by artifact hunters,
it's just like I could see their spirits.
Yes, I knew they were around.
They were standing right next to me.

Honor the dead. They were once just like you and me.
You know how hard it is to find your way.
It was the same for them. You can help them find their way
back to the Creator
by recognizing only the good things they did while they were alive.
If for some reason we don't go directly back to the Creator,
those who follow us can help show us the way
back to the Creator
by acknowledging us after we leave Mother Earth.
Me, I plan to go directly to the Creator!
I don't know about you.
That's between you and the Creator.

"The Peacemaker sent only
the Instructions of good things.
That's what you follow."

The
Peacemaker

The education that we teach came from the Peacemaker.
It reforms you for the benefit of yourself and your people
so that you may get back to where the Creator is
and that's what He wants.

His plan is for all His people to get back.

Our Instructions say to live off the land and create your own welfare.

We have the story of the Peacemaker.
Part of it is beyond my knowledge
and beyond anybody else's that walks on this Mother Earth.
We know that the Peacemaker was born from a virgin mother.
She had never had anything to do with any man.
But to have a child means that there's got to be a man.
That man had to be the Creator . . . 'cause He said,
"The people are doing wrong on this Earth,
so I must send a message down there."
So he sent the message down to Earth
that a child was going to be born,
one that would carry His message to the people.
So we believe that somehow only the Creator knows how
the creation could come that way.
We believe the Creator is the father of that child.

This child was getting his messages from the Creator.
Just like we are getting it now.
The Creator wasn't down on Earth to tell him what to do.
It was messages that came into his mind.
That's how we are getting the message today.
He was sent down to deliver the message the Creator wanted.
He was just like us, yet he was certainly a special, special baby.
He had powers and it was coming from his father
who was the Creator.
There were things he could do that no other human could do.
For instance, he made a canoe out of stone and made it sail,
which was very unusual.

When he made his stone boat,
his grandmother and his mother were the only witnesses.

As he worked on his canoe, his grandmother was thinking it wouldn't float,
but not his mother.
It was the grandmother that was standing in the back.
She didn't say anything but in her mind she was saying to herself,
"That thing's not going to float. It's made out of stone."
But the Peacemaker had the power to read her mind
even though he was working.
When it was time to put the boat in the water
he was first, then his mother, and next his grandmother followed.
The grandmother was still thinking that the canoe wouldn't float.
He turned around and answered her question, "It'll float."
So he said, "Well, help me push it out."
It was partly on the shore.
So they shoved it off and he got inside.
They sent luck with him on his journey.
None of them besides the Peacemaker and his mother thought it would float
but it did.
The river was strong with big waves.
But because it was made of stone it floated right through.
Just traveled right along.

So on his journeys he was going about
looking for the leaders of all the people
who were fighting each other.
They were all separate, all in different places.
They were not all in one village.
They were all over, maybe a group here or groups over there,
and each one of them had a leader, but they were all evil.
So on his journey, he had to travel over a lot of ground
to get to the leaders.
There were obstacles he had to go through.
For instance, there was a log across the stream.
Some would have to get off and carry that canoe over onto the other side
to bypass this log. But he didn't have to
because he had the power to raise that water.
He had extraordinary power like his father, the Creator.

You or I couldn't do it. We don't have that kind of power.
We'd have had to pick our canoe up and go around it
to bypass the log. He didn't have to.

We call his abilities powers.
To raise the waters to get to where he was going
meant he was powerful.
But doing that was nothing
compared to being able to reform those evil leaders.
He did that, which shows us
that he completed the mission his father sent him to do.
If it hadn't been for what he did for us
none of us would be here today.
All the evil leaders would've eaten all the people.
Then they would have died, too,
because there would be no more people to eat.

One of The Instructions the Peacemaker gave us
was for our leaders.
They were to work for the welfare of the people.
It was not meant for you to build yourself up above the people.
It was for everyone to be equal.
Our leaders don't get paid.
Even I have to make my own living.
So the way I see it with the United States,
it seems to me the leaders are making a living off of the people,
their own people.
That's not going to work and it's not working.

The Creator has a brother. You call him the devil.
We say he's working against the Creator.
You can ask the Creator how that happened.
That's beyond my knowledge. He never told us why.

The Creator made this Earth.
He said this world would be the place for our people.
He gave us our Instructions right after the flood
and we listened.
We didn't know there was land across the water.
But that's where the Peacemaker went
to teach them what was right and what was wrong.
Before the Peacemaker, the people didn't know right and wrong.
But they wouldn't listen to His Instructions. They killed him.
There was nothing wrong for the Indians to do,
so the Creator's brother had to go across the ocean
and bring people over here. He got to the people.
The evil brother said, "I'll control the people."
We didn't have rum and drinks before the white man came,
before the people from Europe came.
They didn't know it was wrong.
That's why they came here and brought rum and Bibles,
fiddles and gambling with them.
So when the devil brought over the people,
he brought the seeds for the evil.

The Creator is telling you to do good things.
It's harder to do good than bad
because the devil makes you think his message
is stronger than the Creator's.
The evil brother says that he is going to control the people.
And he's trying hard to do that,
but the Creator is sending the message of what is right and wrong
to give you a chance to fight against the devil.

The Creator made the world with all these things on Earth
and created "Human Beings." He didn't create the evil, though.
The devil did make some things on Earth.
What he put here you'd not want to eat.
It will make you sick or even take your life.

It's a life of jealousy, greed, and evil.
That's his way of taking your mind off the Creator,
off doing good.
He's happy when you take another life.
Doing that is supposed to make you feel like you have power,
even power to take a life. That's what evil does.
It fools you to make you think you have that power.
But only the Creator really has the power.

Right now is an important time. Changes are coming.
The earth is trying to replenish itself and the people could help.
I don't think they will,
because making and hoarding money is behind everything.
I say let's stop making the cars, stop the industry, and let's purify the Earth,
but they're not going to do it because of money.
That would take a lot of sacrifice.

You know what He tells us!
You must live off the land, which means you've got to plant.
That's where you get your nourishment.
Nobody seems to have the time to touch the earth;
nobody is willing to put their hands into the soil.
How can you know anything important unless you do that.
You want to know The Instructions! Start with the Earth.

You got Instructions too, but you put Him on the cross.
He never got to finish His Instructions.
So you don't know what the future is
because you never heard all that He was going to tell you.
He went there to give instructions and they killed Him.
I don't know if Jesus was a Jew or what, but He came to us.
We knew Him as the Peacemaker.
When He left here He went across the waters
to give instructions like He gave us.

What He told us became our way of life.
We listened and did as He asked.

My people do our ceremonies all the time,
three seasons, giving thanks to the Creator.

It is a must that we do them.
We've got to show our appreciation.
There can be no end to doing them,
or He's going to take the food away from us.
Like with our strawberry ceremony;
right now there's only a few berries left.
There'll be a time when we'll have to use a substitute.

So why did the Creator pick us
to entertain His son, the Peacemaker?

Why couldn't they get somebody else out there
to entertain Him? I guess it was because
nothing happened to Him while He was here with us.
But when He went across to give the Instructions to others,
they killed Him before He could finish.
When He returned to us, He came back as a person.
Only He could do that, we can't.
When He came back we had to entertain Him.
That's why we say we are His people.
We are the Creator's children.
The Peacemaker left The Instructions of what we must do
to demonstrate to the Creator we knew.
These Instructions tell us what to do to entertain the Creator.
      Still doing that right up to now.
      That's what part of the Mid Winter ceremony is.
      We've got a lot of things we have to do,
      but part of it is to entertain the Creator.

When the Peacemaker finished giving us The Instructions
He planted the tree of peace
and made us bury all our weapons used to make war
under the tree. That was the white pine.
We were never to fight again
because He said that if we used the good mind
we could work out our differences.
Even then there was no word for warrior in our language.
There still isn't.

"Nobody can get away from the Creator.
It can't be done.
He's a part of everything, even us."

Origins

I don't know about anyone else's Instructions.
I just know mine.
Soon there's going to be new Instructions.

There's going to be a new instructor for the purification.
We were saved during the last purification.
We'll be going back to the place we came from
and be saved again. I know how,
but we don't really tell, because we know
that the archeologists and anthropologists
would be going into the place
and searching. So we don't tell.

I'll give you a hint. When I speak I tell where we came from.
It was from a long way to the south.
If you want to know about our ceremonies and knowledge,
you have to go further than what you call the United States.
I think it was in South America
because the people started walking.
This maybe was near the beginning
and they were told by the Creator's people to start out.
I don't know what happened.
Some went west, some east; others went more to the south.
Many traveled north over many, many years.
I think this was the longest walk.
Then there was another splitting up into all the Four Directions.
One day we were promised we'd all get back together.
That's not taken place yet, but it will.
In the Creator's time we'll all be back together.
That's what the Hopi talk about, too.
This is what I mean when I say
that all the Indian people came from that place.

The Haudenosaunee, my people,
went east after coming up from the south.
We're supposed to go back and tell what we saw in the east.
But we never went back that we can remember.
That was taken away from our minds
so we wouldn't give it away.

We've been back but we don't remember it.
The Hopis say that all the people will come back together
and that has begun already.
At the time of purification
the Creator will give us our memories back.

Today is all I have. It's all anybody's got.
I can't go back to any time in my life except in my memories.
There's no going into tomorrow, I can't even think about it
because the memories haven't been made yet.
That's why I'm content doing whatever comes up.

Today we have people who are great teachers.
Some of them see visions.
These things you can't get from reading.
That's why when I talk, I can only talk about my vision.
I've been shown what it feels like
when people are not ready
and when the world's going to start to change.

"Everybody is on a path.
What you think about the most
tells you which path you are on.
The best path is the spiritual one.
It's the only one that helps you
become a Human Being."

Prophecies

My spirit travels when I sleep.
In a dream I was shown things.
The Creator showed me.
The maples started dying from the top down.
The rivers traveled backward and fish died.
Volcanoes erupted one after another.
Huge hurricanes killed thousands of people.
Earthquakes shook the world
and destroyed everything where they hit.
Then the great winds like people had never seen before
fell from the sky. Then I saw a drop of blood
just about to fall like rainwater dripping off a roof.
I knew in my dream it was a plague carried in the blood
and it would kill lots of people.
Then the fire came and burned all over the Earth.

When I finally woke up I had an awful feeling.
I was left with just the grief.
I had such a feeling of emptiness.
It was like there was nothing.
One minute in the dream I was right at the edge of a cliff
and then I was falling down and that was the end of my life.
I saw my kids and my family all at the end
but there was nothing on the Earth.
There was no rain to cleanse the Earth.
There were no plants, no animals, and nothing to eat.
Everything was burned. It was the end.
When I woke up, oh, I was glad it was just a dream.
I know the dream was telling me what was coming,
but there's still time left.
Maybe people will wake up like I did from the dream
and do the things needed to bring back the balance.
I'm doing what I can to get the message out.
When it's almost time for the world to come to an end,
The Creator is going to send his helpers down here to pick up seeds.
You got to have seeds to plant again.

We know there's going to be a purification.
The last purification was by water.
My people were placed at the center of the Earth,
deep underground.

We were given a warning that time
to go into the mountains.
My ancestors were told what to do and the people did it.

This time the Creator's going to cleanse Mother Earth by fire.
No one will escape the fire,
except those who followed the Creator's Instructions.
All those with the good mind will end up where the Creator is.
Those that make it to the spiritual world
after the earth is burned by fire
will come back to life. The spirit will go back into the body.
It will be like they'll be waking up and coming back to life.
It will be like the Earth and all the life on it
will be starting all over again.
There will be a new world.

This time the message is
that the people have to have a clean mind and a clean body.
There will be signs of what's coming.
First thing is that the Creator will take care of the children Himself.
If they're born, they won't stay long before he takes them back.
Also, He'll take care of the old people so they won't see.
All those that fought for Mother Earth, they'll go up in the sky.
All those that fought a long time ago
and died fighting for the Earth,
they're going to be waking up from the dead.
They won't have to go through the fire.
They'll be taken to the Creator's place.

The real path goes to the Creator.

That's the one you've got to be on. It's the one with meaning.

And that's the one our ceremonies are all about.

They help to keep us connected to the Creator.

If you're looking for your path, look for the Creator.

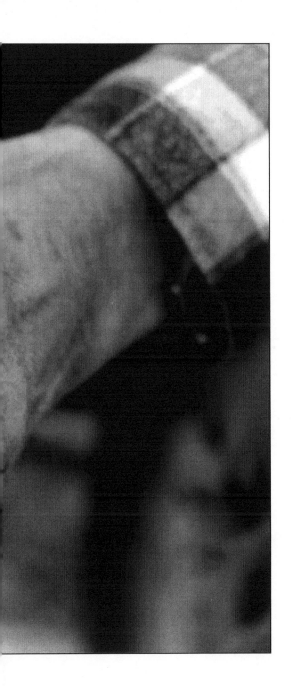

"If you are looking for your path,
look for the Creator.
If you ask how to find your path,
that means you aren't on it.
The people who are on their path
don't have to ask."

The Path

Think about Him and think about the creation.
Once you do that, you'll start getting your Instructions.
You don't have to think too hard about it.
It's not something you reason out,
it's something you do.
It's so simple.

There is no security other than in the spiritual.
No one can separate himself from the spiritual
because nobody can take the Creator out of himself.
It's always there trying to guide us.
If we don't listen all the time, we head for trouble.
It's important that we recognize we are spiritual people.
Once we do that, it's easier to start listening.
The Creator likes to talk to us.

I've heard people pray.
They do it at ball games.
They start meetings with prayers.
There are a lot of prayers said out loud in churches.
They have a guy that prays to start up the Congress
and that's what he's paid to do.
I don't know if he's there for anything else.
Just says a prayer!
There are a few "thank yous" in there,
but mostly it's a lot of asking.
They say "Bless us, Father,"
"Protect us, Lord,"
"Take care of us and guide us."
They ask for even more than that,
but I can't remember everything
because it's so much.

I don't know why they ask for anything.
The Creator's already done it all.

And He's doing it all the time.
All we've got to do is look around to know that.
The Creator just wants us to give our thanks.
I don't know why some people pray out loud.
I can't pray for anybody and nobody can pray for me.
It's just between Him and me or you and Him.
I burn tobacco so that my words of thanks
will reach the Creator. I can do that for you,
but I can't give Him your thanks.
You have to do that for yourself.
You don't really have to get me to burn tobacco for you.
You can even do that for yourself.
Nobody is closer to the Creator than you are yourself.

You can get off your path
and think you're separated from the Creator,
but you're not.
You can get back on your path
and feel closer to Him, but that's a feeling.
Nobody can get away from the Creator.
It can't be done. He's a part of everything, even us.
It's like with your mother and father.
You can run away from them.
You can be ashamed of them.
You can deny you came from them.
But you can't get away from coming from them.
They're always there in you.
That's the way it is with the Creator.
You came from Him because He made you
and He's always looking out for you.

Our helpers are the four Protectors the Creator gave us
to watch over us. They are watching over me right now.
They do that for only certain ones who will ask for it.

The Creator gave us his four Protectors
to look out for us. They're like spirits.
We can call on them in times of trouble.
They're always there for us.
We don't have to call the Creator
because He has given us the help we need.
For that we are thankful.
We are to be helpers, too.
We are responsible for looking out for others,
the two-legged and the four-legged.
We've also been instructed
to protect the plants and the waters.
If we don't do our duty as The Instructions say we should,
then the Protectors may forget about us.
Everything has its duty.
We "Human Beings" do too.

I know the Protectors exist. I talk to them.
Some people call them guardian angels.
They try to tell us things to help us.
We have to learn to listen.
Just because you can't see them
doesn't mean they're not there.
Some people can and do see them; they're our seers.
If we look hard enough, we can start seeing them, too.
But seeing them is not as important as listening to them.
Once you can hear them, you'll never be the same again.
Your life will change.
That's what the Creator wants for us.
That's part of His plan.
It was always meant for us to hear them,
but somewhere along the way we tried to hide our spirituality.
We've missed out on a lot the Creator had prepared for us.
This is the time for us to start listening again.
It's in the prophecy.
The people will hear and see the Protectors once again.

But there are some people who don't know about the four Protectors.
The Protectors are here with us now.
You communicate with them by burning sacred tobacco.
A lot of people ask me to burn tobacco
and call on the helpers when they go to the hospital.
What happens to them or their family depends on the Peacemaker.

There are only circles in nature, which is life.
That means there is no beginning, no end.
There's no end, you just go back to the beginning.
There is a center, though. You could travel here and there,
go way around and come back
and you'd be at the center.
That means that the center is everywhere.
Common sense, huh!
You get it.
You're the center then.
Doesn't that make sense?
If you're the center, you have the power of the Creator
when you do good for the people.
Each person has that same power.
When all the people use that strength together
they can help restore Mother Earth and all the people will benefit.
There would be no need for the purification.

There are no straight lines in nature.
There are no squares.
That means there is nothing to box us in.
We are free. The Creator made it that way for us.
He did make circles, however.
The Earth is a circle.
Go to the ocean and you can see the horizon.
You know right there that the world's not flat;
it's round and so is the sun and the moon.
Life's not flat either.
Our lives are circles.

We come from the Creator and we go back.
There's another circle you better not forget.
Everything you do comes back to you.
Do good and it comes back good.
Do bad and it comes back, too.
Try to do more good than bad.
Your time here will be better.

Power belongs only with the Creator.
That's the only power there is.
A person can think he has power
but those kind of people come and go.
Only the people themselves remain.
It's the people who will decide who will lead them.
They will take a bad leader for only so long,
then they wake up.
Sometimes when they do, there is turmoil and killing.
But it's the people who always win out.
That's why the people should always use the good mind
when selecting their leaders.
They should never be swayed with empty words and promises.
They must listen with the heart
because that's where the Creator speaks.

Our government has been called a democracy
because everyone gets to participate.
Our chiefs cannot force anything on the people.
They can make suggestions and offer solutions to problems,
but they cannot force the people to accept it.
The final decision is theirs.
I guess that's why it's considered the oldest running government in the world.

Our leaders are marked. It's because of their path.
What was out in front of them

was there from the beginning.
They came from the Creator that way.
Everybody has a path, some paths are harder than others.
That's why our chiefs never wanted to be leaders.
They knew it would be bumpy. No matter what they do
there's always some who go against them,
maybe even hire the spirits to get at them.
So they never asked for the job,
but the elders were watching
from the time they were only so high.
The elders could see who they were and what path they were on.

To be a chief you can't want it.
If a man wants to be chief
that means he wants power.
It's up to the clan mother to decide
who will be chief. If she sees a man desiring the position,
she passes him over because he wants it for himself
and he might not work for the good of the clan.
So she goes to the one who doesn't want to be chief.
She knows if he's picked, he will use the good mind
and work for the good of his people and not himself.

Someday the people will be shown
that they have no power at all
and it's nature that will show them.
You cannot control nature. You have to live with it.
That's where the harmony comes in.
Anyone who doesn't believe it will have to be shown
that they don't really have any power except through the Creator.

Make only the promises you're going to keep.
If you slip and mess up, straighten it out as fast as you can.
If you don't, it will hurt you and you'll be so sad.

Evil is something you do that's wrong.
Some call it sin.
You sin when you go against the Creator,
The Instructions. You can sin by thinking.
If your thoughts are not pure, you are sinning.
If I tell you I like you when I really hate you,
I am doing wrong. You're sort of hiding.
When you're pretending, you are working for the evil.

You can sin when you destroy the Earth.
You're going against The Instructions.
Those who do evil think they are using their own mind.
But they're not. The devil is coming into their mind
and giving them Instructions.
But if the mind is strong on positive things,
then you will not follow The Instructions of the bad mind.
The Peacemaker sent only The Instructions of the good things.
That's what you follow.

You can be stopped from getting to the Creator
by hating or hurting people.
Everything that's negative will lead you away from the Creator.
Everything that's positive helps guide you on your path to the Creator.
Good is the thing to follow.

At times some people get disturbed at the actions of others.
They talk about them and say bad things about them.
When somebody does something against somebody else,
I know they've lost their way.
They tell me that by the way they act.
I don't ask questions about why they do what they do
and we aren't supposed to judge. All I know is
they belong to the Creator, too.
We all make mistakes but none of us are alike.

It takes time for some people to learn.
It's harder for some to get on their path
and harder still for others to stay on it.
We're all different, but there's a path for everybody
whether you see it or not.
It's always in front of you.
Anyway, what kind of world would this be
if there were no people in it?

The way you live tells everybody
what kind of person you are.
Your actions speak for you.
You can talk all you want, but
everybody around already knows who you are.
Treat others kindly, and you'll never have to say a word.
Somebody is always watching. They'll want to be like you
and you'll never have to open your mouth.
Through you the world will be more peaceful.
It's not a hard job. Just follow The Instructions
the Creator gave to us.

Respect is what the people have for you
when you don't abuse your power.
Nobody can take your power away from you;
only you can give it away.
When you don't exercise your power in a positive way,
then the people will not have any respect for you.
If nobody has respect for you, then nobody'll be listening
when there's a need for you to let your power work
for the good of the people. Your words will be hollow
and no ears will be open,
even if what you say is for everyone's good.

It is up to us how we treat other people.
We decide if we will live in peace

or if we will be fighting each other.
If we're always fighting, then
we will be bringing disease and sicknesses on ourselves.
It is better to live in peace
and that way we will be living with good health.
We are always the ones making decisions
as to what it will be for us.
We have to understand that we have something to do
with how our lives will turn out.
It is better to live in harmony.
Peace should be our goal, our way of life.
It is up to us to practice it.

Every road is an adventure.
Your education is waiting for you on every trip you take.
If you never go anywhere you'll never know
all the things the Creator has prepared for you.
With each person you meet
there's a special gift for you to have.
It's another piece of the puzzle
that will help you sort out your place in the circle.
It will be of use to you during the remainder of your life.
Miss one of the people you are supposed to know
and there will be a hole. That will leave you with a question
that will be hard for you to find an answer for.
You will always be wondering what was left out.
I'm always anxious for the next trip. When I get restless,
everybody says, "Leon's wanting to go again."
They're always right.
I don't want to be wondering about what I missed.

The Creator made sure that we had a way to get in touch with Him.
He left us a sacred plant and said that if we would burn it,
He would see the smoke and open His ears to hear what we had to say.
Whenever we pray we use the sacred tobacco

and the smoke carries our words to the Creator's place.
Some Indians put it in a pipe and light it.
Then it's passed around the circle for everyone to smoke.
Among the Iroquois we put some in the stove in the Longhouse.
It doesn't matter how it's done, our words are still carried on the smoke.
He sees the smoke, opens His ears and hears what we say.
Mostly we give thanks and He knows the rest.

There's no need to worry.
The Creator's upset when we worry
because He's able to take care of everything.
If we worry then He knows we're not relying on Him.
Whatever concerns you doesn't matter
because it will work out the way it's supposed to be.
Your worry doesn't change anything;
it just delays things
from working out
the way the Creator planned all along.
There are things that worry can do.
It can make you take your mind off your path.
It can make you sad while you're waiting to see what's going to happen.
And it can make you have illnesses,
sometimes that can shorten your life.
All those things displease the Creator.
You could be about more important matters
for the benefit of the people.

Pain is your lookout, like a scout.
It's a signal that tells you to watch out
because something is going on.
When you have anger or you hate somebody
or you could even feel slighted, that emotion settles inside.
If you let it stay there, it's going to cause you trouble.
It's important that you stay in the balance
with the Creator and the environment.

When you do that, you can have healthy relations
with everything around you.
A lot of times the pain will go away.
If it's been there a long time,
you've got to get some help to take it away.
People go to the reader for that.
They've got those abilities
because the Creator doesn't want you to kill anybody,
not even yourself.
I'd say it's better not even to kill yourself.
It would be easier on you to stay in the balance.
You'll be happier here and in the hereafter.

It's even in our Instructions that a man can't be a chief
if he has killed.
People don't understand what they're doing when they take life.
The person who does it is in for trouble
even if they're never caught.
The Creator knows.
Our Instructions say that the one who does it
gets all the dead person's karma.
They have theirs and the other person's, too.
The one who dies is relieved of their karma
and goes straight to the Creator's place clean.

I know about killing.
That's what happened to my daughter.
We think her man did it
because he took off.
Nobody could find him, but I know where he is.
I wouldn't want to be him. He's facing a lot up ahead.
He's got all his karma from before and now
the killing along with her karma.
The here and the hereafter is on him.

I miss her.
I'd like it if she could just come by for a visit occasionally,
but she's not with us anymore.
Her son's been living with us since then.
He was little when it happened, but he still really misses her.
People tell me I should go after that man.
They say they'd get him for what he did
and worry about the hereafter later.
I'm not like that.
I don't hate him; that's just not in me.
He'll get what's coming to him.
He created his own revenge.
I'm staying out of it,
because I don't want to be attached to him in any way.
Whatever happens to him is between him and the Creator.

As long as there is hunger and poverty,
there is work to do. The spiritual way

is to change the systems
so that all human beings can live with dignity
and live in peace and harmony.
We can bring that about if we work to make it happen.
You've got to work for the good.
I'm working for the Creator.
I refuse to take part in anything
that would destroy what He has made.

It's a privilege to walk on the Earth.
We should walk in such a way
as to never leave our footprints.
That will protect the Earth for the generations to come.
What will they do when they come
and find that the Earth will not provide for them
because of what we did!
Maybe they wouldn't be able to live long enough
to clean up the mess we made
just so they could have a place to live.
Think how sad you'd be
if you knew your grandchildren suffered
because of what you did.

Steve Wall 91

Carolyn DeMeritt

Steve Wall has written and photographed more than a half-dozen books about Native American wisdom and spirituality, including *Wisdom's Daughters* (with Harvey Arden, HarperPerennial, 1994) and *Wisdomkeepers* (with Harvey Arden, Beyond Words, 1990). His journeys in search of indigenous spiritual elders have taken Wall around the world, and as a photojournalist he has covered stories in more than forty countries. His work has been published in *National Geographic*, *Time*, *People*, *Smithsonian*, and other national media. He has appeared on CBS-TV's News Sunday Morning, FOX-TV's Crier Report, and NPR radio's Diane Rehm Show.

Hampton Roads Publishing Company

. . . for the evolving human spirit

Hampton Roads Publishing Company
publishes books on a variety of subjects including
metaphysics, health, complementary medicine,
visionary fiction, and other related topics.

For a copy of our latest catalog,
call toll-free, 800-766-8009,
or send your name and address to:

Hampton Roads Publishing Company, Inc.
1125 Stoney Ridge Road
Charlottesville, VA 22902
email: hrpc@hrpub.com
www.hrpub.com